Pearls of Wisdom

African and Caribbean Folktales

The Integrated Language Skills
Workbook

Raouf Mama and Mary Romney
Illustrations by Siri Weber Feeney

PRO LINGUA  ASSOCIATES

Pro Lingua Associates, Publishers
P. O. Box 1348
Brattleboro, Vermont 05302 - 1348 USA
E-mail: prolingu@sover.net
www.ProLinguaAssociates.com
Office: 802 257 7779
Orders: 800 366 4775
SAN: 216-0579

*At Pro Lingua
our objective is to foster an approach
to learning and teaching that we call*
interplay, *the* **inter***action of language
learners and teachers with their materials,
with the language and culture,
and with each other in active, creative
and productive* **play**.

Copyright © 2001 by Raouf Mama and Mary Romney

ISBN 0-86647-136-7

This book was designed by Arthur A. Burrows and set in Bookman Oldstyle, a modern, bold adaptation of a traditional square serif face, with Arab Brushstroke, a caligraphic display type; these are both Agfa digital fonts. The front cover is by Siri Weber Feeney. The book was printed and bound by Capital City Press in Montpelier, Vermont.

Printed in the United States of America
First printing 2001. 1500 copies are in print.

Contents

User's Guide

This **Workbook** is a supplement to the main text, *Pearls of Wisdom, African and Caribbean Folktales: The Listening and Reading Book.* The workbook contains a variety of activities that provide for work in all skill areas (speaking, listening, reading, writing) and vocabulary development. Each unit of the workbook follows this pattern of activities:

1. Pre-listening
2. Listening
3. Summarizing
4. Reading: Vocabulary
5. Re-telling
6. Writing and Speaking: Reflecting
7. Connecting
8. Concluding

The workbook offers the best way to achieve maximum learning and full enjoyment and appreciation for the folktales in **The Listening and Reading Book.**

Answers to the summarizing and vocabulary exercises are in the back of the workbook so that you may use these exercises as out-of-class homework, as well as in-class activities.

There is also a **glossary** of terms following this User's Guide. These terms are used in each unit, and so it would be advisable to be sure that the terminology is clear and fully understandable.

The collection of folktales is also available as **a Cassette Recording** featuring the voice of Dr. Raouf Mama, the collector of these stories and an established Griot — a masterful West African story teller. The stories on the cassette follow the stories in **The Listening and Reading Book** word-for-word.

Glossary
of terms used in the lessons

The following is a list of terms that are used in the lessons. These are words that are generally used to discuss and write about literature.

Character — a person or an animal in a story; a person or an animal that a story is written about.

Characteristic — quality of a person or a thing; way of describing a person or a thing.

Culture — the system of beliefs and values shared by you and your community, and the behaviors determined by that system; the collective word for the principles and beliefs upon which behavior, education, religion, all forms of art, and social relationships are based.

Metaphor — a symbol; one thing expressed as something different.

Moral — what the story teaches you about the theme; a lesson the story teaches, expressed as a sentence; advice the story gives you, usually expressed as an imperative sentence and said or written at the end of the story.

Proverb — a sentence that usually gives advice or expresses wisdom; Proverbs are usually old and are passed from generation to generation over long periods of time. A proverb is similar to a moral, but instead of being quoted at the end of a story, it is usually spoken as advice about a specific situation.

Symbol — one thing used in representation of another.

Symbolize — use one thing to represent another.

Synonym — a word with a similar meaning to another word.

Theme — the central concept the story illustrates; the central idea around which the story revolves, expressed as a phrase.

Value — a guiding principle to live by; a principle that guides your thoughts and behavior; a belief.

Pearls of Wisdom

African and Caribbean Folktales

The Integrated Language Skills
Workbook

How Chameleon Became A Teacher

Benin

1. Pre-listening

You will hear a story about a crocodile and a chameleon. Before you listen to the story, discuss the answers to these questions with your classmates.

What do you know about crocodiles?
What do you know about chameleons?
What is your definition of a friend?
What is a test of true friendship?

2. Listening

Before listening to the story, read the following questions.

What kind of relationship did Crocodile and Chameleon have?
What did they often do together?
What did Crocodile offer Chameleon?
What did Crocodile tell his family?
When Crocodile went to meet Chameleon, what did Chameleon do?
What did Chameleon's test of Crocodile prove?
After testing Crocodile, what did Chameleon learn?

While listening to the story, listen for the answers to these questions.

After listening, discuss the answers to the above questions.

Finally, listen to the story again.

3. Summarizing

A. Complete this summary of the story with the following words:

talking   **honest**   **invited**   **threw**   **realized**   **friends**   **bit**   **taught**

Chameleon and Crocodile were good _friends_. They often spent long periods of

time _____ together. So when Crocodile _____ Chameleon

to dinner at his house, Chameleon happily accepted the invitation. But Crocodile was

not _____ with Chameleon. Crocodile told Chameleon to jump into the lake so

that he could take Chameleon to his house. But instead, Chameleon _____

a stick into the lake. Crocodile _____ the stick, thinking it was Chameleon.

When Chameleon saw this, he _____ how important it was to test Crocodile.

This _____ him a very valuable lesson in life.

B. Now read the story and check your summary.

4. Reading: Vocabulary

A. Match the words and phrases from the story with the words or phrases that have a similar meaning by writing the letter corresponding to the synonym. *(Numbers in parenthesis refer to the paragraph number.)*

Word or words from the story   **Synonym**

_e_ was (very) fond of *(1)*   a. jumped into water, headfirst
____ sunbathing *(1)*   b. an especially delicious food
____ nodding *(1)*   c. very large; enormous
____ delicacy *(3)*   d. moving the head in agreement
____ gigantic *(4)*   e. enjoyed
____ dived *(4)*   f. lying in the sunshine

B. Look at these definitions and then write one of these words on the following blank.

guest   **trembling**   **splash**   **wisdom**   **fled**

Definition	Word from the story
the effect of something falling in the water *(4)*	_____
shaking with fear *(5)*	_____
ran away in fear *(5)*	_____
an invited person *(5)*	_____
intelligence, understanding and common sense *(6)*	_____

2

C. Write a sentence using a form of each of these words.

1. to be fond of _____

2. to nod _____

3. to splash _____

4. delicious _____

5. enormous _____

6. to tremble _____

7. to flee _____

8. wise _____

- *The answers to exercises 4 and 5 are at the back of the book starting on page 60.*

5. Re-telling

A. Re-tell the story in your own words.

B. Re-write the story from Crocodile's point of view: Use "I" for the crocodile.
   For example, *My name is Crocodile. I live at the bottom of a lake.* etc.

6. Writing and Speaking: Reflecting

A. The Moral of the Story

"Look before you leap." Is this the moral of the story?
Is there more than one moral to the story?
Is a moral explicitly stated in the story?

What does the story teach?
Do you believe in what the story teaches?
Would you teach the lesson of this story to your child?
If so, tell or write about how you would teach this lesson to your child.

3

B. **The Theme of the Story: Values**

Is there more than one theme in this story?
What is/are the theme(s)?

Which of these phrases expresses the theme of the story?

the need for caution even in familiar territory
the need to test even close relationships

What are the values the story teaches?
When you were a child, did you learn the values in this story?
If so, who taught them to you?

Tell or write about how you learned the values in this story.

C. **The Theme of the Story: Culture**

How does this story compare to the values in your culture?
Tell or write a folktale from your culture about friendship.
Tell or write a folktale from your culture about deception.

D. **Related Proverbs**

Proverb: *When in Rome, do as the Romans do.*

What does it mean? How is it related to this story?
Do you think this is good advice? Why? In what situations?
Are there any similar proverbs from your culture?

7. Connecting
. . . to your experience

What does it mean to "take on the local color?"
Do you believe in doing this?
If you have been an immigrant or a visitor to another country, have you ever tried
 to "take on the local color" in your new environment? Why or why not?
If you have observed foreigners in your country, do they "take on the local color?"
Do you think they should? Why or why not?

Tell or write about deception between friends that you have experienced or observed.

8. Concluding — Symbols and Metaphors

As you answer these questions, think back to what you know about chameleons and crocodiles and what you read in the story.

What does Crocodile symbolize in this story?
What does Chameleon symbolize?

Are any other animals symbols of these same qualities?

Are there any other common metaphors for these qualities in your culture?
If so, what are they?

Why Hawk Preys on Chicks

Nigeria

1. Pre-listening

You will hear a story about a chicken, a hawk, and some other animals. Before you listen to the story, discuss the answers to these questions with your classmates.

What do you know about hawks?
What do you usually think about when you think of chickens?
What is a good way to resolve conflict within a community?
What can happen when you let others make decisions for you?

2. Listening

A. **Before** listening to the story, read the following questions.

What was Hawk's relationship to all the other animals?
What did all the other animals want Hawk to do?
What did Hawk want the other animals to do?
Did Chicken attend the meeting with all the other animals?
What did the animals discuss at their meeting?
What was the conclusion of the animals at their meeting?

B. **While** listening to the story, listen for the answers to these questions.

After listening, discuss the answers to the above questions.

Finally, listen to the story again.

3. Summarizing

A. Use the words below to fill in the blanks in the following paragraph. The completed paragraph is a summary of the story.

attend	decide on	preyed on	message
sacrifice	except for	volunteer	meeting

Long ago, all the birds and animals were friends, _____*except for*_____ Hawk, who always _____ small animals and their young ones. Then one day, the animals sent a _____ to Hawk to tell him not to hunt them anymore. Hawk agreed to stop if the animals could _____ one who Hawk could hunt. None of the animals wanted to _____ to be Hawk's food, so they decided to have a _____ to discuss what to do. Chicken was the only animal who did not _____ the meeting. She had said that she would accept whatever decision the other animals made. So they decided to offer Chicken and her chicks as a _____ to Hawk. Hawk accepted the decision, and that is why Hawk preys on chicks.

B. Now read the story and check your summary.

4. Reading: Vocabulary

A. Use these words to complete the sentences below.

squabbling	promptly	exception	sacrifice
congratulating	victim	arena	relief

1. Hawk was the only _____.

2. . . . they did not know who to offer as a _____.

3. The animals were arriving at the public _____.

4. There was much _____ and no agreement.

5. . . . who should be offered to Hawk as a sacrificial _____.

6. Shouts of joy and _____ filled the air.

7. The animals jumped up and down, _____ each other.

8. Hawk _____ agreed to the decision.

6

Why Hawk Preys on Chicks

B. Vocabulary for baby animals and adult animals. In the story, Chicken's young are called "chicks." In English, sometimes the words for baby animals are different from the words for the same animal as an adult. Look at the list below:

Adult animal	Baby animal
chicken	chick
lion	cub
dog	puppy
cow	calf
cat	kitten
bear	cub
deer	fawn
pig	piglet
sheep	lamb
goat	kid

Now cover up the right hand column and try to make this sentence for each animal.

A baby _____ is a _____.

C. In the story, the animals have a meeting. In this exercise you will practice with words for the different situations in which people speak to each other: one person speaking to many, two people speaking to each other, a small group of people speaking to many, many people speaking to each other, etc.

Fill in the blanks with the following words in the sentences below. The first one is done for you. You may need to use the same word more than once.

conference	conversation	lecture	address
meeting	discussion	speech	colloquium

1. At the beginning of every semester, the President of our college gives a welcoming *speech* to all the new students. Her _____ is usually about 20 minutes long.

2. We just had our monthly staff _____, which is always attended by everyone in our department. But next week, we're going to have a special _____ to plan the move to our new office.

3. I really enjoyed Professor Johnson's _____ this morning. Sometimes it's hard to take notes in his classes, but today he was easy to follow, and very interesting.

4. Every spring I attend an annual _____ on bilingual education. About 5,000 linguists and educators from all over the world attend.

5. Last night I called an old friend of mine. We had such a nice _____, reminiscing about our high school days.

6. Email is great. People all over the world can have a written _____ about something without being face-to-face. Any number of people can participate.

7. Next spring, I'm going to be a panelist on a _____ at a conference for English teachers. The subject will be how computers affect language education.

7

D. In the story there are several different verbs that are similar to the meaning of "conflict." The animals have a squabble during their meeting in the arena. "Squabble" is one word used in the story to mean "conflict." Circle the words in this list that are "conflict" words.

argument	**war**
young	**smooth**
fight	**agreement**
discuss	**debate**
disagreement	**decision**
battle	**satisfied**
stare	**prey on**

- *The answers to exercises 3 and 4 are at the back of the book starting on page 61.*

5. Re-telling

A. Re-write or re-tell the story from Hawk's point of view. Use "I" for Hawk.

B. Re-write or re-tell the story from Chicken's point of view. Use "I" for Chicken.

C. Imagine Chicken had gone to the meeting. How would the story have ended? Re-write or re-tell the story with all the animals present at the meeting.

6. Writing and Speaking: Reflecting

A. **The Moral of the Story**

What is the moral of the story? What does the story teach?
Do you believe in what the moral teaches?

B. **The Theme of the Story: Values**

How are the themes of foresight, responsibility, and teamwork related to the story?
What are the values represented in the story? Do you agree with these values?

C. **Related Proverbs**

Which of these is the best proverb for the story? Why?

Proverbs: *Take responsibility for your own destiny.*
Don't leave for tomorrow what you can do today.
Don't leave in the hands of others what you can do for yourself.
Sing your own part in the choir.

What does each proverb mean? How is it related to the story?
Are there any similar proverbs from your culture?
If so, tell them to your classmates and explain them.

7. Connecting
. . . to your opinion

How do you feel about hunting and other sports involving animals?
Are you a vegetarian? Why?
Do you think people should hunt animals as a sport?
Should some animals be hunted and not others?
What sports involving animals are popular in your country?
Do you think it's important to protect animals?
If yes, which ones? Why?

8. Concluding — Symbols and Metaphors

As you answer this question, think back to what you know about hawks.
What does Hawk symbolize?

Think again about problem-solving in communities.
What does Chicken symbolize?

Pearl of Wisdom

Gabon

1. Pre-listening

You will hear a story about a little boy, his mother, and a king. Before you listen to the story, discuss the answers to these questions with your classmates.

> Are names of children important to parents?
> Who should have the right to name children?
> How do you respond when someone is unfair to you?
> What is a tyrant?
> Have you ever lived in a country where a tyrant ruled?
> Have you ever had to fight against tyranny?

2. Listening

A. **Before** listening to the story, read the following questions.

> Was the king kind or cruel?
> What was his rule on names of children?
> How did Pearl of Wisdom prove that his name was appropriate?
> What was the King's reaction when he discovered his name?
> What did Pearl of Wisdom's mother do?
> What was the mother's solution?
> How did the king change as a result?

B. **While** listening to the story, listen for the answers to these questions.

After listening, discuss the answers to the above questions.

Finally, listen to the story again.

10

3. Summarizing

A. The sentences below form a summary of the story, but they are not in the correct order. Put the sentences in the correct order by writing a number from 2 to 8 on the line next to each sentence. The first one has been done for you.

_____ But one little boy in the kingdom was named Pearl of Wisdom.

_____ The king was amazed by his intelligence, so he wanted to know more about him.

_____ In turn, the mother of Pearl of Wisdom gave the king an impossible task.

__1__ Once there was a powerful king who named all the children in his kingdom with ugly, insulting names.

_____ He was so intelligent that he won the king's riddle-solving contest.

_____ The king decided to punish the mother of Pearl of Wisdom for giving him that name, so he gave her an impossible task.

_____ This made the king realize how unfair he had been, and he allowed people to name their own children freely.

_____ When the king asked his name, and he answered that it was Pearl of Wisdom, the king became very angry because he hadn't named him.

B. Now read the story and check your summary.

4. Reading: Vocabulary

A. Match the words from the story with their synonyms or phrases on the right, by writing the letter corresponding to the synonym. *(Numbers in parenthesis refer to the paragraph number.)*

Word from the story   **Synonym or Definition**

__e__ wisest *(1)*   a. authority of a king; government of a king
_____ tyrant *(1)*   b. crying
_____ reign *(2)*   c. a specific job or responsibility assigned to a person
_____ mean *(2)*   d. pick the fruit or vegetables on a farm
_____ pretended *(2)*   e. most intelligent
_____ exceedingly *(4)* f. small grains from a plant that grow to become a new plant
_____ ignored *(10)*   g. disobeyed; not paid attention
_____ merciful *(10)*   h. made a false impression
_____ harvest (v) *(11)* i. holding something tightly in the hand
_____ weeping *(12)*   j. a person who governs in a cruel way
_____ task *(12)*   k. extremely
_____ clutching *(13)*   l. kind; generous; compassionate
_____ seeds *(14)*   m. cruel; abusive

11

B. Fill in the blanks with the appropriate form of the correct expression below.

go back on one's word   **behind one's back**   **spare one's life**
                    in vain   **break the law**

1. You can always count on my brother. When he promises to do something, he always does it. He never _____. He's straightforward with everyone. He never says one thing _____ and then another thing to your face.

2. I'm a public defender, a lawyer that represents clients who cannot afford to pay for legal services. I routinely defend people who _____. Recently, I defended a man who had committed a violent crime. I pleaded with the judge not to sentence my client to death. But my pleas were all _____. The judge did not want to _____. So my client was sentenced to death.

- *The answers to exercises 3 and 4 are at the back of the book starting on page 62.*

5. Re-telling

Re-write or re-tell the story from the mother's point of view.

6. Writing and Speaking: Reflecting

A. The Moral of the Story

Which one of these statements best serves as the moral for this story?

Never accept unfair treatment.
Always defend your own beliefs.
Have faith in yourself and faith in what you are doing.

Can you think of another sentence that expresses the moral of this story?
Is there a character in the story that symbolizes the moral?

What does the story teach?
Do you believe in what the moral teaches?
If so, have you had any experiences in your life that have taught you this same lesson?

B. **The Theme of the Story: Values**

What is the theme of the story?
Do you think that either of these phrases expresses the theme?

> the fight against tyranny
> the power of individual freedom

Are these the only themes? Can you think of others?

What are the values represented in the story? Do you agree with these values?

C. **Related Proverbs**

Proverbs: *A victory against tyranny is freedom for all.*
The most powerful ruler shares power.

What do these proverbs mean? How are they related to the story?
Which one is the most relevant to the story?

Are there any similar proverbs from your culture?
If so, tell them to your classmates and explain them.

7. Connecting
... to your experience and your country

National leaders:
Do you know of any countries that are governed by leaders like the king in this story?
Have you ever lived in a country that was governed by a leader like the king in this story?
Does your country have a royal family?
If so, what is the role of the royal family?
Do they have direct contact with the people of your country?
What is their relationship to the government?
Does your country have a president? a prime minister?
Are you familiar with royal families of other countries?
Which royal families do you admire? Why?

... to your country and culture

Naming:
In your country and culture is the naming of children very important?
Are there any rules, traditions, or beliefs about naming children?
Are only certain names allowed?
In your country and culture, do names mean something?
In English, it is common to name girls after flowers. For example, Lily, Daisy,
    Rose, Heather, Violet, Laurel, Jasmine, etc. Is this common in your language?
What are girls named after in your country and culture?
Pearl of Wisdom is named after a personal quality. In your country and culture,
    is it common to use personal qualities as names?

8. Concluding — Symbols and Metaphors

As you answer these questions, think again about tyranny.
What does the king symbolize in this story?
What do Pearl of Wisdom and his mother symbolize?

13

Anancy and the Guinea Bird

Antigua

1. Pre-listening

You will hear a story about a spider and some other animals. Before you listen to the story, discuss the answers to these questions with your classmates.

What animals are famous for setting traps?
What do you think about when you think of spiders?
What does it mean to "mind your own business?"
What are natural disasters?
What is a drought?
What is the effect of a drought on a country and its people?

2. Listening

A. **Before** listening to the story, read the following questions.

Why was Anancy hungry?
What did Anancy ask the Father God to do?
What happened to the animals who asked Anancy a question?
What did Guinea Bird do to make Anancy ask about him?
What happened to Anancy when he asked about Guinea Bird?

B. **While** listening to the story, listen for the answers to these questions.

After listening, discuss the answers to the above questions.

Finally, listen to the story again.

3. Summarizing

A. The sentences below form a summary of the story, but they are not in the correct order. Put the sentences in the correct order by writing a number from 2 to 9 on the line next to each sentence. The first sentence is done for you.

_____ He got the idea of asking the Father God to make a new law: whoever does not mind their own business by asking questions will die.

_____ He provoked Anancy. Instead of minding his own business, Anancy asked a question about Guinea Bird.

_____ He was the only one who had food when everyone else was starving.

__1__ There was a terrible drought in the land where Anancy lived, so there was no food for anyone.

_____ So Anancy got fat by eating them as they died.

_____ Anancy had to think of a way to trap some food for himself.

_____ Anancy got many animals to ask him questions, and they all died as a result.

_____ Guinea Bird realized that all the animals would die if Anancy continued, so he decided to trap Anancy in the same way as Anancy was trapping all the other animals.

_____ As soon as Anancy asked the question, he died just like all the other animals who had asked him.

B. Now read the story and check your summary.

4. Reading: Vocabulary

A. Match the words from the story with their definitions on the right, by writing the letter corresponding to the definition. (Numbers in parenthesis refer to the paragraph number.)

Word from the story	Synonym or Definition
_____ chipping *(7)*	a. deception; dishonesty
_____ grunted *(9)*	b. disappear gradually
_____ fatal *(9)*	c. not see; not notice; not pay attention
_____ trap *(9)*	d. trick or deceptive action with no possible escape for the victim
_____ trickery *(10)*	e. in an elegant way; royally
_____ bald *(11)*	f. breaking something large into small pieces by using an axe or other tool
_____ majestically *(14)*	g. deadly; resulting in death
_____ ignore *(15)*	h. made a short, deep sound, like a pig
_____ fade *(16)*	i. without hair on one's head

Anancy and the Guinea Bird

B. In the story, Anancy lives in a land that suffers from a drought. A drought is one kind of natural disaster. Below are some other examples of natural disasters and where they occur.

Land	*Land and water*	*Mountains*
forest fire	**hurricane**	**avalanche**
flood	**earthquake**	**landslide**
tornado	**volcanic eruption**	
drought	**tsunami**	

Now fill in the blanks in the definitions that follow.

1. The sudden movement or shaking of the land is a(n) _____. Buildings, roads, and bridges are usually destroyed as a result.

2. Large areas of trees are burned in a(n) _____. The result is the destruction of a wooded area.

3. An extremely large wave or series of waves in the ocean is a(n) _____. It is usually caused by an earthquake on the ocean floor.

4. The violent and fast movement of wind in a circular motion is a(n) _____. It looks like a spiral column moving across a large area of flat land, destroying everything around it.

5. When rocks and soil which are usually stable fall down the side of a mountain, they produce a _____.

6. Violent tropical rain combined with very severe winds blowing at very high speeds is a(n) _____.

7. When there is no rain for a long time where it usually rains, there is a(n) _____. Without water from rain, the land is very dry, so plants, crops, animals, and people die.

8. When the land is covered by too much water from rain or melting snow, there is a(n) _____.

9. An explosion inside the earth through the top of a mountain or the sea floor is a(n) _____.

10. When large amounts of accumulated snow slide down a mountain unexpectedly, they produce a(n) _____.

16

Anancy and the Guinea Bird

C. In the story, Guinea Bird sings about his "hair." Many animals do not have hair, as humans do. There are many other words for the exterior or the skin of animals. Some of them are listed below. After each word, write an animal that has this kind of exterior. You may need to use a dictionary.

Exterior or Skin   Animal(s)

a. shell   _____

b. fur   _____

c. scales   _____

d. hide   _____

e. feathers   _____

f. skin   _____

• *The answers to exercises 3 and 4 are at the back of the book starting on page 63.*

5. Re-telling

Re-write or re-tell the story from Guinea Bird's point of view.

6. Writing and Speaking: Reflecting

A. The Moral of the Story

Which of these statements best serves as the moral or this story?

Be careful what tricks you play on others, for they might be used against you.
Be careful not to get caught in your own trap.
Mind your own business.

What does the story teach?
Do you believe in what the moral teaches?

B. The Theme of the Story: Values

What is the theme of the story?
What are the values represented in the story? Do you agree with these values?

C. Related Proverbs

Proverb: *Practice what you preach.*

What does this proverb mean? How is it related to the story?
Are there any similar proverbs from your culture?
If so, tell them to your classmates and explain them.

7. Connecting

. . . to your experience and your country

Have you (or has your country) ever experienced a natural disaster?
Describe it and explain its effects on the country and the people who experienced it.

Have you ever lived in a country that was affected by a drought?

Look back at the list of natural disasters in a previous exercise.
How many of these occur in your country?

Are some kinds of natural disasters more common than others in your country?

Are there different kinds of natural disasters in different parts of your country?

Does one kind of natural disaster scare you more than another? Explain why.

. . . to your country and culture

What is the difference between asking questions from curiosity and interfering with
other people? Give examples.

In your country and culture do people participate in the lives of their neighbors, or do
they lead individual lives?

What are the questions you cannot ask a stranger? For example, age? income?
religion?
What are the questions you cannot ask someone older than you?
What are the questions you cannot ask non-members of your family?
What are the questions you cannot ask a person of the opposite sex? For example,
marital status? age?

. . . to another tale

Compare this tale to *"How Yogbo the Glutton Was Tricked."*

8. Concluding — Symbols and Metaphors

Think again about spiders and about animals that set traps.
What does Anancy symbolize in this story?
What does Guinea Bird symbolize?

How Goat Moved to the Village

Haiti

1. Pre-listening

You will hear a story about a goat and a hyena. A lion is also one of the characters in the story. Before you listen to the story, discuss the answers to these questions with your classmates.

What do you know about hyenas?
What do you know about lions?
How do animals behave when they are hungry?
Did you ever have to escape from a dangerous situation?
What are some reasons why people migrate?

2. Listening

A. **Before** listening to the story, read the following questions.

What was Goat doing when Hyena arrived?
What does each character in the story want to eat?
How did Goat avoid being eaten by Hyena?
When did Goat go to the village from the jungle?

B. **While** listening to the story, listen for the answers to these questions.

After listening, discuss the answers to the above questions.

Finally, listen to the story again.

3. Summarizing

A. Use the verbs below to fill in the blanks in the following paragraph. The completed paragraph is a summary of the story.

ran away	offered	realized	came along
ran after	arrived	feared	escape
	discovered	buy time	

One day, Goat was baking sweet potatoes, when Hyena ___came along___.

Goat _____ Hyena some food but he quickly _____ that

Hyena wanted to eat him, not the food. Goat _____ for his life, so he

thought of a strategy to _____ so that he could find an escape from Hyena. Goat's strategy was to eat his sweet potatoes slowly. While Hyena was waiting for

Goat to finish the sweet potatoes, Lion _____. Lion said he wanted Goat to

finish eating so that Hyena could eat Goat and he could eat Hyena. Hyena

_____ he was in terrible danger, so he _____.

Lion _____ him. Goat saw that this was his chance to _____

the jungle, so he went to live in the village.

B. Now read the story and check your summary.

4. Reading: Vocabulary

A. Match the words from the story with their definitions on the right, by writing the letter of the definition beside the word. (Numbers in parenthesis refer to the paragraph number.)

Word from the story

_____ harvest (1)
_____ ashes (2)
_____ bite (3)
_____ struggling (6)
_____ clawing (10)
_____ howled (11)
_____ chewed (11)
_____ fierce (15)
_____ numb (17)

Definition

a. aggressive scratching by an animal
b. without feeling
c. cried; shouted
d. used the teeth to grind food
e. tear, or hold something with the teeth
f. food produced from plants on a farm
g. intensive; violent; angry or strong
h. making a strong and difficult effort
i. the material left after something has burned completely

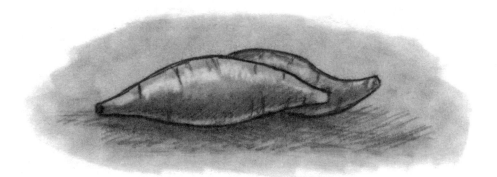

B. Use the expressions below to fill in the blanks in the following sentences.

help yourself   **all over**   **just in time**

itching to (do something)   **blood-chilling**   **once and for all**

1. Hyena arrived at the exact moment Goat was preparing to eat. He came
   _____ to eat with Goat.

2. Goat wanted to be polite and generous with his food, so he invited Hyena to serve
   himself, saying "_____."

3. Hyena was very impatient with Goat because he was extremely hungry. His hunger
   was almost uncontrollable. He was _____ eat Goat.

4. When Hyena realized that Lion wanted to eat him, he was so terrified that he
   reacted physically. He was numb with fear _____ his body.

5. Lion arrived with a thunderous, _____ sound that shocked and
   scared Hyena and Goat.

6. After listening to Goat's story, Lion soon became impatient and wanted to finalize
   everything so that _____ he could eat.

• *The answers to exercises 3 and 4 are at the back of the book starting on page 64.*

5. Re-telling

Re-write or re-tell the story from Goat's perspective.
Re-write or re-tell the story from Hyena's perspective.

6. Writing and Speaking: Reflecting

A. The Moral of the Story

What is the moral of the story?
What does the story teach?
Do you believe in what the moral teaches?

B. **The Theme of the Story: Values**

How is the theme of fairness related to the story?
Do you think Hyena and Lion were unfair?
What would have been a fair solution?
How is the theme of peaceful co-existence related to the story?
What are the values represented in the story? Do you agree with these values?

C. **Related Proverbs**

Proverb: *Live and let live.*

What does this proverb mean? How is it related to the story?
Are there any similar proverbs from your culture?
If so, tell them to your classmates and explain them.

7. Connecting
. . . to your experience

Did you ever have to leave your home or your country because your were in danger?

Goat thought that Hyena was unfair and Hyena thought that Lion was unfair.
Have you ever been in a situation that you thought was unfair to you? Explain.

Have you ever been in a dangerous situation with an animal?

Have you ever had to plan an escape?

Hyena was terrified when he realized that Lion was planning to eat him.
Have you ever felt so terrified that you couldn't react?

Have you ever seen one animal hunt or kill another animal?

. . . to your country and culture
Food:
In your country and culture, do people eat meat or are most people vegetarian?
What are your favorite foods in your country?
When people from other countries visit your country, what foods should they try?
What do most of the farms produce in your country?
If you are living in a foreign country, how have you adjusted to the new food?

8. Concluding — Symbols and Metaphors

What do each of the animals symbolize in this story?
Do you think it is possible for animals to live together peacefully without hurting
    each other?
Do you think it is possible for people to live together peacefully without hurting
    each other?

The Greedy Father

Benin

1. Pre-Listening

You will hear a story about a father and his daughter. A monkey is also one of the characters in the story. Before you listen to the story, discuss the answers to these questions with your classmates.

What is greed?
Can you give any examples of greed?
What are the usual consequences of greed?
What do parents usually look for in the future spouses of their children?
Who should decide who you marry? You, or your parents?
What's more important in a marriage? Material wealth or love and happiness?

2. Listening

A. **Before** listening to the story, read the following questions.

Why did Nadjo want his daughter, Gbessi, to get married?
Did a lot of men want to marry Gbessi? Why?
What did men do when they proposed to Gbessi?
What was Nadjo's reaction when men proposed to Gbessi?
How did Nadjo react when Monkey proposed to Gbessi?
Why did Nadjo and Gbessi accept Monkey's proposal of marriage?
What happened soon after Monkey married Gbessi?
How did Monkey transform Gbessi?
How did Nadjo react to Gbessi's transformation?

B. **While** listening to the story, listen for the answers to these questions.

After listening, discuss the answers to the above questions.

Finally, listen to the story again.

23

3. Summarizing

A. The sentences below form a summary of the story, but they are not in the correct order. Put the sentences in the correct order by writing a number from 2 to 12 on the line next to each sentence. The first sentence is done for you.

_____ All the young men of Nadjo's village proposed to Gbessi and offered gifts to Nadjo, but Nadjo and Gbessi rejected all the young men.

_____ Shocked at her husband's transformation, Gbessi tried to escape from him, but Monkey ran after her, following her to her father's house.

_____ He wanted to find a husband for Gbessi because he wanted to receive a high bride-price.

_____ Monkey married Gbessi and they went to live on a farm.

_____ When she finally got to Nadjo's house, she turned into a monkey as he watched.

__1__ Nadjo, a poor man, had a beautiful daughter, Gbessi.

_____ He convinced Nadjo to let him marry Gbessi.

_____ Monkey heard about the beautiful daughter and the greedy father, so Monkey decided to marry the daughter.

_____ He suddenly turned himself back into a monkey.

_____ This broke her father's heart, and he soon died.

_____ Monkey's friends gave him lots of presents and made him very wealthy. Then, Monkey transformed himself into a handsome man.

_____ But farming was hard work, and Monkey soon got tired of his new life, and missed his life as a monkey.

B. Now read the story and check your summary.

4. Reading: Vocabulary

A. Match the words and phrases from the story with their synonyms on the right, by writing the letter corresponding to the synonym. *(Numbers in parenthesis refer to the paragraph number.)*

Word from the story	Synonym or definition
_____ crumbling *(1)*	a. dense concentrations of trees and bushes
_____ endure *(11)*	b. very sad, disappointed, disillusioned
_____ interminable *(11)*	c. motivated by a strong force or need
_____ realized *(13)*	d. shrunken and wrinkled
_____ driven *(13)*	e. crazy, mentally unstable
_____ thickets *(14)*	f. endless, very long
_____ compound *(15)*	g. suddenly understand
_____ grimaced *(15)*	h. a residential area for one family, including a house, garden, guest house, etc.
_____ withered *(15)*	i. deteriorating, disintegrating
_____ heartbroken *(15)*	j. tolerate
_____ insane *(16)*	k. expressed pain on the face

The Greedy Father

B. The following words are all related to marriage. Write the correct words for the definitions. Use your dictionary if necessary.

marry	bride	groom	wedding
marriage	propose	bride-price	spouse

_____:
at a wedding, the man who is getting married

_____:
at a wedding, the woman who is getting married

_____:
husband or wife, general word for either gender

_____:
the ceremony that celebrates the first day of a marriage

_____:
ask a woman to be your wife, or ask a man to be your husband

_____:
the amount of money paid to the woman's father by the man who wants to marry the woman

_____:
enter into a legal union with a person in order to become his wife or her husband

_____:
a formal relationship with a person, as his wife or her husband

C. Fill in the blanks with the words below.

marry	bride	proposed
marriage	wedding	groom

My fiance and I are planning to get married next year. He _____ to me last summer and I said "yes" immediately because he is the kind of man I have always wanted to _____. He is generous, intelligent, creative, and hardworking. Both of us have large families, with many brothers and sisters, so we're planning a big _____ in the garden of my uncle's country estate. Although the minister of our church will perform the wedding, we are planning to write our own vows. We want our _____ to be a long and happy one. I'm not planning to dress as a typical _____. I'm going to wear a non-traditional wedding gown that I designed. But my fiance wants to be a typical _____, so he'll wear a tuxedo. He's more traditional than I am.

The Greedy Father

D. Select the correct synonym or definition for the words underlined in the sentences below. The paragraph numbers for the underlined words are in parenthesis at the end of the sentence.

1. <u>Countless</u> young men proposed to Gbessi. *(2)*

   a) a few
   b) none
   c) very, very many; too many to count

2. The young men offered <u>provisions</u> to Nadjo as part of the bride-price they were ready to pay. *(2)*

   a) farming equipment
   b) supplies of food
   c) money

3. Gbessi was a very <u>obedient</u> daughter. *(3)*

   a) did exactly what her father wanted her to do
   b) did the opposite of what her father wanted her to do
   c) did only what she wanted to do

4. Nadjo was very <u>greedy</u>. *(title)*

   a) generous
   b) only thought of his daughter and not himself
   c) never satisfied and always wanted more and more

5. Monkey brought <u>gorgeous</u> <u>fabrics</u> to Nadjo. *(6)*

   a) very ugly   a) clothes
   b) ordinary   b) textiles for making clothes
   c) very beautiful   c) gifts

6. Monkey brought <u>priceless</u> gifts to Gbessi and Nadjo. *(6)*

   a) cheap
   b) without value
   c) extremely expensive and valuable

7. Monkey said that all the gifts he brought were only a <u>token</u> of his love for Gbessi. *(8)*

   a) a small coin
   b) something stolen or robbed
   c) a small part of something big

8. Monkey missed <u>chattering</u> with the other monkeys in the jungle. *(11)*

   a) talking happily and rapidly
   b) laughing and joking
   c) having fun

9. Gbessi ran <u>swiftly</u> away from Monkey. *(14)*

    a) very fast
    b) fearfully
    c) without direction

10. In the end, Gbessi realized she had married a <u>hideous</u> monkey instead of a handsome prince. *(13)*

    a) extremely ugly
    b) attractive
    c) deceptive

- *The answers to exercises 3 and 4 are at the back of the book starting on page 65.*

5. Re-telling

Re-write or re-tell the story from Gbessi's point of view.
Re-write or re-tell the story from the Monkey's point of view.
Re-write or re-tell the story from Nadjo's point of view.

6. Writing and Speaking: Reflecting

A. The Moral of the Story

What is the moral of this story? Is it explicitly stated?
What does the story teach?
Do you believe in what the moral teaches?

B. **The Theme of the Story: Values**

Which of these phrases best expresses the theme of the story?

the corrupting power of money
how greed can blind a person

What are the values the story teaches?
Would you teach the values of this story to your child?
If so, tell or write about how you would teach them.

When you were a child, did you learn the values in this story?
If so, who taught them to you?

Tell or write about how you learned the values in this story in your life.

C. **Related Proverbs**

Proverbs: *You can't tell a book by its cover.*
All that glitters is not gold.
Money is the root of all evil.

Explain the meaning of each proverb and how these proverbs relate to the story.

Is there a proverb from your country and culture that relates to this story?
If so, tell it to your classmates.

7. Connecting
. . . to your country and culture

Courtship in your country

How do you attract the attention of eligible bachelors/ladies?
    (For example, do people usually put advertisements in the newspaper?)
How does a man propose to a woman?
What considerations do people make before marrying in your culture?
What do you think is the best age for marriage for a man? for a woman?
What is the typical age for a woman to marry in your country? for a man?

Marriage

What is an arranged marriage?
Are there arranged marriages in your culture?
What are the advantages of arranged marriages?
What are the disadvantages of arranged marriages?
If you are not living in your country, is courtship different in the country where you
    are living now?
Who should choose your spouse — you or your parents?

Weddings in your country

Who performs the wedding ceremony?
Is special food/drink served?
Are weddings expensive?
What kinds of presents do couples receive?
Is clothing very important?
What do couples wear?
What does it symbolize?
Is jewelry important?
What are the important symbols in a wedding ceremony?
Is religion important in weddings?
Do couples take vows?
What vows do couples take?

. . . to another story

Compare the greed in *"The Prince and the Orphan,"* with the greed in *"The Greedy Father."* What is the result of greed in each case?

8. Concluding — Symbols and Metaphors

As you answer these questions, think back to your ideas on greed and the consequences of greed.

What does Nadjo, the father, symbolize?
What does Monkey symbolize?

Why Cat and Dog are Always Fighting

Cape Verde

1. Pre-listening

You will hear a story about a cat and a dog. A monkey is also an important character in the story. Before you listen to the story, discuss the answers to these questions:

When you think about the relationship between cats and dogs, what comes to mind?
Do you think cats and dogs can get along well together?
When you think of monkeys, what characteristics come to mind?
How would you describe your relationship with your best friend?
Did a friend of yours ever become your enemy?
Have you ever been robbed? How did you feel?

2. Listening

A. **Before** listening to the story, read the following questions.

Originally, what kind of relationship did Cat and Dog have?
What did they find while they were searching for food?
How did they get the cheese?
Why did they take the cheese to Monkey?
What did Monkey do with the cheese?
Why did Cat and Dog start fighting?

B. **While** listening to the story, listen for the answers to these questions.

After listening, discuss the answers to these questions.

Finally, listen to the story again.

3. Summarizing

A. The sentences below form a summary of the story, but they are not in the correct order. Put the sentences in the correct order by writing a number from 2 to 10 on the line next to each sentence. The first sentence has been done for you.

_____ So they decided to consult Monkey.

_____ While searching, they suddenly smelled some fresh cheese.

_____ Cat and Dog blamed each other for losing the cheese to Monkey, and since then, they have been fighting.

_____ Then they stole the cheese from the house.

_____ But instead of dividing the cheese equally, monkey ate it all himself.

_____ They found the house where the smell was coming from.

__1__ For many years, Cat and Dog had been best friends.

_____ They were hungry and looked for food everywhere.

_____ After they got the cheese, they couldn't decide how to divide it.

_____ Then one year, there was a terrible famine in their village.

B. Now read the story and check your summary.

4. Reading: Vocabulary

A. Match the words from the story with their definitions on the right, by writing the letter corresponding to the definition. *(Numbers in parenthesis refer to the paragraph number.)*

Word from the story	Definition
_____ famine *(2)*	a. a device for weighing things
_____ searched *(2)*	b. intelligence; good judgment
_____ aroma *(5)*	c. moved the tongue to wet the lips
_____ sniffed *(5)*	d. destroy; cause destruction
_____ ruin *(9)*	e. a sweet, pleasant smell
_____ argue *(10)*	f. characteristics that make a person famous
_____ licked *(11)*	g. verbally disagree
_____ scales *(13)*	h. looked for; tried to find something
_____ reputation *(16)*	i. smelled
_____ wisdom *(16)*	j. many people starving

• *The answers to exercises 3 and 4A are at the back of the book starting on page 67.*

Why Cat and Dog are Always Fighting

B. All the words in the list below refer to vocal sounds that people and animals make. Some of the qualities of each sound are indicated in the chart.

	sad	pain	loud	soft	angry	high	low
whimper	●	●		●		●	
bark			●				
whisper				●			
yelp		●	●			●	
pant				●			
growl				●	●		●
scream		●	●		●	●	
hiss				●	●	●	
moan	●	●		●			●
mew				●		●	
screech		●	●		●	●	
howl	●	●	●			●	
cry	●	●	●		●		
shout			●		●	●	

Which ones do you think are usually only animal sounds?
Which ones are usually only human sounds?   Which ones can be both?

Look up the unfamiliar sounds in your dictionary.

C. Now try to use these sounds in a sentence.

whimper   _____

bark   _____

whisper   _____

yelp   _____

pant   _____

growl   _____

scream   _____

hiss   _____

moan   _____

mew   _____

screech   _____

howl   _____

cry   _____

shout   _____

5. Re-telling

Re-tell the story from Monkey's point of view.
Re-tell the story substituting every instance of greed and deception with honesty and generosity, and substituting a happy ending.

6. Writing and Speaking: Reflecting

A. The Moral of the Story

What is the moral of the story?
Do you agree with the moral of the story?
What does it mean to be outsmarted?
What lessons does the story teach?

B. The Theme of the Story: Values

Which of the following do you feel is the theme of the story?
    compromise and agreement
    trust and betrayal
    deception
What values do you think the story teaches about each of these possible themes?
Do you know about a situation that was similar to the one in the story?
Have you ever been the victim of someone else's greed?
Do you share the values represented in this story?

C. The Theme of the Story: Culture

How do you feel about sharing what you have with other people?
Is sharing important in your culture?

D. Related Proverbs

Proverb: *Do unto others as you would have them do unto you.*

What does this proverb, called "The Golden Rule," mean?
How does this proverb relate to the story?
Is there a similar proverb in your culture?

7. Connecting

. . . to your personal experience

Have you ever been robbed or deceived by someone?
If so, what was stolen from you?
How were you deceived?
What was the consequence?
Have you ever lost a friend because of a disagreement?
What did you disagree about?

. . . to other individuals and groups

Do you know of any other long-time conflicts between individuals?
Do you know of any other long-time conflicts between groups?
How old are these conflicts?
How could these conflicts have been prevented?
Are these conflicts similar to the one between Cat and Dog?

. . . to another story

How is this story similar to the story of Monkey and Leopard?
What do you think Monkey and Leopard would tell Dog and Cat?

8. Concluding — Symbols and metaphors

As you answer these questions, think about what you know about cats and dogs.

What do Cat and Dog symbolize?
What does the cheese symbolize in this story?
What does Monkey symbolize?

A Fisherman and His Dog

Puerto Rico

1. Pre-listening

You will hear a story about an old fisherman, Don Manolito, and his dog. They live on the island of Puerto Rico, where he is a fisherman. One day there is a big storm.

What do you think about when you think of dogs?
What are some of the positive characteristics of dogs?
Why do you think people have dogs?
Have you ever had a dog? If so, describe your relationship with your dog.
If you have never had a dog but you know about a relationship between a person and a dog, describe that relationship.
What do you know about storms in the Caribbean or other tropical areas ?

2. Listening

A. **Before** listening to the story, read the following questions.

What was Don Manolito's occupation?
Who was Don Manolito's only close friend?
What did Taino do whenever Don Manolito went fishing?
Where was Don Manolito when the storm started?
Where was Taino when the storm started?
Did Don Manolito return to San Juan after the storm?
How was Taino transformed?
What is the eternal symbol of Don Manolito's friendship with Taino?

B. **While** listening to the story, listen for the answers to these questions.

After listening, discuss the answers to these questions.

Finally, listen to the story again.

3. Summarizing

A. The paragraph below is a summary of the story, but it contains some incorrect words. Cross out the incorrect words and replace them with the correct ones. The first correction is done for you as an example.

Don Manolito was an old fisherman who lived in ~~Santo Domingo~~ *San Juan* with his donkey, Taino. Don Manolito had many close friends, including Taino. Taino always followed Don Manolito everywhere. Nobody in the town was accustomed to seeing Don Manolito and Taino go to the seashore in the morning and return in the evening. One day, a terrible tsunami occurred while Don Manolito was out at sea. Taino waited on the seashore for Don Manolito to come back from fishing. But when Don Manolito did not return, Taino swam out to an island off the shore to wait for him. Fishermen went out to where Taino was, but when they arrived, they saw that Taino had been transformed into ice. And up to this day, the figure of Taino waiting for Don Manolito remains off the seashore, as a tribute to their friendship.

B. Now read the story and check your corrections in the summary.

4. Reading: Vocabulary

A. Match the words from the story with their definitions on the right, by writing the letter of the definition beside the word. *(Numbers in parenthesis refer to the paragraph number.)*

Word from the story	Synonym or Definition
_____ hut *(1)*	a. a reaction of surprise at something incredible
_____ broken-hearted *(1)*	b. first light of the morning
_____ ashore *(5)*	c. consumed; swallowed; destroyed
_____ dawn *(9)*	d. a very small, simple house, with one or two rooms
_____ amazement *(10)*	e. disillusioned shock, sadness, and fear
_____ dismay *(12)*	f. spoken evidence; declaration; statement
_____ overwhelmed *(13)*	g. sad; made to feel sad because of something or someone
_____ testimony *(13)*	h. from the water toward the land

B. Find the word or phrase that matches the definition and write it in the space on the right. Look for the word or phrase in the paragraph indicated.

Definition	Word/Phrase in the Story
disappeared *(5)*	_____
losing brightness; darker *(5)*	_____
being very violent *(5)*	_____
an electrical explosion in the sky, producing a flash of light, usually during a rain storm *(7)*	_____
very tall; very high *(7)*	_____
beach; the land next to the sea *(7)*	_____
carried by a powerful force *(7)*	_____

- *The answers to exercises 3 and 4 are at the back of the book starting on page 68.*

5. Re-telling

Re-tell or re-write the story from Taino's point of view.
Re-tell or re-write the story from the point of view of the man who found Taino.

6. Writing and Speaking: Reflecting

A. The Moral of the Story

What is the moral of the story?
What does the story teach?
Do you believe in what the story teaches?

B. The Theme of the Story: Values

Which of these ideas best expresses the theme of the story?
> *the power of friendship*
> *loyalty*
> *self-sacrifice*

What values do you think the story teaches about each of these possible themes?
Do you share the values represented in the story?

C. The Theme of the Story: Culture

Do you think friendship is important?
How do you define friendship?

D. Related Proverbs

Have you ever heard the expression *"a dog is man's best friend?"*
Do you agree with it?
Do you think dogs can be better friends than people?

7. Connecting
. . . to your opinion about animals

A. Add another pet to the row of animals — perhaps a pet that is popular in your country.
Add two more adjectives to the column of character traits.
Then decide which character traits belong to each pet, and put a check mark in the row and column according to your opinion about each animal.

	dogs	cats	horses	birds	fish	monkeys	hamsters	_____
intelligent								
communicative								
interesting								
friendly								
warm								
independent								
trainable								
beautiful								
loyal								
_____								
_____								

B. Write or speak about why you selected specific character traits for each animal.

. . . to your personal experience

Pets:
What characteristics make a good pet?
What animals have these qualities?
Does Taino have any of these qualities? Which ones?
What is the best pet to have? Why?
Have you ever had a dog? If so, what did your dog have in common with Taino?

Friendship:
What are the qualities that make a good friend?
Describe the qualities of your best friend.
What's the difference between family and good friends?
Is friendship important in your country and culture?
What would you do for a friend that you wouldn't do for anyone else?

Statues and monuments:
In the story, Taino turns into a statue and becomes a kind of monument.
How would you name this monument? Here are two possible names:

The eternal wait
Man's best friend

Think of two other names for this monument.

Are there any monuments in your country or your hometown that you especially like?
What do they commemorate?
Draw a picture of your favorite monument and show it to your classmates and
    explain what or who it honors.

8. Concluding — Symbols and Metaphors

As you answer these questions, think again about the relationship between dogs
    and people.
What does Taino symbolize in this story?
Could another animal substitute for the dog in this story? Why or why not?

What does the storm symbolize?

How Yogbo the Glutton Was Tricked

Benin

1. Pre-listening

You will hear a story about Yogbo, who is a glutton and a trickster. The story is also about Alougba, a young girl. Before you listen to the story, discuss the answers to these questions.

> Imagine you were kidnapped. What would you do to escape?
> What is a glutton? What's the difference between a hungry person and a glutton?
> What is a trickster? Can you trust a trickster?
> What's the best way to teach a trickster a lesson?

2. Listening

A. **Before** listening to the story, read the following questions.

> What was Alougba doing when Yogbo trapped her?
> After Yogbo trapped Alougba, where did he put her?
> What was the real voice of the singing drum?
> What was the message of the song from the drum?
> How did Alougba's parents free her from Yogbo?
> What happened to Yogbo after his drum stopped singing?

B. **While** listening to the story, listen for the answers to these questions.

After listening to the story, discuss the answers to the above questions.

Finally, listen to the story again.

3. Summarizing

A. The sentences below form a summary of the story, but they are not in the correct
order. Put the sentences in the correct order by writing a number from 2 - 11 on
the line next to each sentence. The first sentence is numbered for you.

_____ When Yogbo woke up and took his drum to another village, and advertised
his singing drum, the drum sang no more.

_____ She became thirsty and stopped to drink water from a hole in a tree.

_____ In the meantime, Yogbo went from village to village advertising his singing
drum, and demanding payment in food and wine from anyone who wanted to
hear the drum sing.

__1__ Alougba was a hard-working little girl who enjoyed going to the forest to get
firewood.

_____ Yogbo realized he had been tricked and escaped from the village.

_____ When her hands got stuck in the hole, Yogbo freed her.

_____ But then he put her inside his drum.

_____ One day she got more wood than she could carry.

_____ One day Yogbo went to Alougba's village without knowing that it was where
her parents lived.

_____ Alougba's parents offered him food and wine, so he ate and drank an enormous
amount, and then he fell asleep. While he was sleeping, Alougba's father took
her out of the drum.

_____ While Alougba was inside the drum, she sang a song that was a call to her
parents to free her.

B. Now read the story and check your summary.

4. Reading: Vocabulary

A. Match the words from the story with their definitions on the right, by writing the
letter of the definition beside the word. The first word is done as an example.
(Numbers in parenthesis refer to the paragraph number.)

Word from the story	Definition
__i__ chore *(1)*	a. completely wet; soaked
_____ foolishly *(2)*	b. in extreme need
_____ drenched *(2)*	c. defenseless; without protection
_____ desperate *(3)*	d. in a deceptive way
_____ plunged *(4)*	e. stupidly; without thinking clearly
_____ helpless *(4)*	f. unpleasant; rough
_____ trap (n) *(5)*	g. escaped
_____ reached *(8)*	h. a thing or a plan to catch someone
_____ captive *(12)*	i. routine work; responsibility; duty; task
_____ cunningly *(13)*	j. a captured person; prisoner
_____ harsh *(16)*	k. quickly and forcefully put one thing inside another
_____ fled *(17)*	l. arrived at a place

B. In the following sentences, fill in the blanks with the words and expressions below.

glutton	**left behind**	**common sense**	**patch up**
keep up with	**got stuck**	**demanded**	**marvel**

1. Hurry up! If you don't walk faster, you won't be able to _____ the others and you will be _____.

2. I'm going to take my jacket to a tailor to see if he can _____ this hole in the sleeve.

3. Instead of politely asking for an explanation of his bill, he got angry and _____ to see the manager immediately.

4. My professor is a brilliant man, but he has no _____. For example, he uses his typewriter instead of his computer.

5. I always _____ at the way children can learn languages so much faster and easier than adults.

6. My cat chased a mouse into a small opening in the wall and then _____ inside and couldn't get out.

7. He wants and eats everything. What a _____!

• *The answers to exercises 3 and 4 are at the back of the book starting on page 69.*

5. Re-telling

Re-tell the story from Yogbo's point of view.
Re-tell the story from Alougba's point of view.
Re-tell the story from Alougba's parents' point of view.

6. *Writing and Speaking: Reflecting*

A. **The Moral of the Story**

Which one of the statements below best expresses the moral of this story? Why?

> *Don't be greedy, for you may one day be the victim of your own greed.*
> *Don't be deceptive, for you may one day be the victim of your own cunning.*
> *Don't allow your own greed to blind you.*

Do you think the story teaches a lesson?

Would you teach the lesson of this story to your child?
If so, tell or write about how you would teach this lesson to your child.
Would you use different characters or examples?

B. **The Theme of the Story: Values**

What is the theme of the story?
Choose the statement that you think best expresses the theme of the story:

> *the consequences of greed*
>
> *the consequences of deception*
>
> *the victory of honesty over deception*
>
> *the use of cunning to defeat cunning*

What are the values represented in the story? Do you agree with these values?
When you were a child, did you learn the values in this story?
If so, how did you learn them?

C. **The Theme of the Story: Culture**

What do you think this story reflects about the culture it comes from?
Tell or write a story from your culture about greed or about cunning.

D. **Related Proverbs**

Proverb: *What goes around comes around.*

What does this mean? How is it related to the story?

Are there any similar proverbs from your culture?
If so, tell them to your classmates and explain them.

7. Connecting

. . . to your experience

From your direct experience, or from your past observations, tell or write about a greedy person.
From your direct experience, or from your past observations, tell or write about a cunning person.

. . . to your opinion

What do you think should be the consequence of greed?
What do you think should be the consequence of cunning?
What do you think of Yogbo's fate?

. . . to your country and culture

In paragraph 13, Yogbo is served many special foods.
In your culture, what are some special foods?
Are there any foods similar to the ones in this paragraph?
Are any of these foods popular in your country?
What are the most popular foods in your culture?
Are some foods or drinks forbidden in your culture?
Have you ever eaten any of the foods in this story?

8. Concluding — Symbols and Metaphors

As you answer these questions, think again about the best way to teach a trickster a lesson.

What does Alougba symbolize in this story?
What does Yogbo symbolize in this story?

Monkey's Argument With Leopard

Congo

1. Pre-listening

You will hear a story about a leopard and a monkey. A tortoise is also one of the characters in the story. Before you listen to the story, discuss the answers to these questions with your classmates.

What do you know about leopards?
What do you know about monkeys?
What is your definition of a promise?
What does "cheating" mean to you? Give some examples of cheating.

2. Listening

A. **Before** listening to the story, read the following questions.

How did Leopard first get himself in trouble?
What did Leopard promise Monkey for Monkey's help?
How did Monkey help Leopard?
What did Leopard do after Monkey helped him?
What did Tortoise get Leopard to do?
Where is Leopard now?

B. **While** listening to the story, listen for the answers to these questions.

After listening to the story, discuss the answers to the above questions.

Finally, listen to the story again.

Monkey's Argument With Leopard

3. Summarizing

A. The sentences below form a summary of the story, but they are not in the correct order. Put the sentences in the correct order by writing a number from 3 to 13 on the line next to each sentence. The first two sentences are done for you.

_____ A group of monkeys were playing near the well and heard him calling for help.

_____ In order to convince Tortoise that the story was true, Leopard jumped back into the well.

_____ Monkey was very angry at Leopard for deceiving him, so he argued that Leopard should free him.

_1_ One day when Leopard was hunting in the forest, he accidentally fell into a well.

_____ Leopard promised the monkeys that he would not hunt them anymore if they helped him.

_____ They told him their story, but Tortoise did not believe them.

_____ When Leopard got out of the well, he grabbed Monkey and said he intended to eat him.

_____ Leopard is still waiting for Monkey to come back and rescue him again.

_2_ Immediately, he started calling for someone to come and rescue him.

_____ The monkeys came to the well and saw how serious Leopard's situation was.

_____ Finally, one monkey rescued Leopard because he believed Leopard's word.

_____ While Monkey and Leopard were arguing, Tortoise came along and asked about their conflict.

_____ Monkey and Tortoise left Leopard in the well.

B. Now read the story and check your summary.

4. Reading: Vocabulary

A. Match the words and phrases from the story with their synonyms and definitions on the right, by writing the letter of the synonym/definition beside the word. The first two are done for you as examples. *(Numbers in parenthesis refer to the paragraph number.)*

Word from the story	Synonym or Definition
_i_ glisten *(1)*	a. serious
_o_ game *(1)*	b. victim, hunted animal
___ flaming *(2)*	c. tolerance, compassion
___ plunge *(3)*	d. very weak
___ predator *(3)*	e. disappear
___ vanish *(3)*	f. strongly encourage, try to convince
___ strife *(5)*	g. pay no attention
___ mercy *(6)*	h. burning
___ ignore *(7)*	i. shine
___ faint *(7)*	j. intensive conflict
___ seek *(8)*	k. fall suddenly and steeply
___ prey *(8)*	l. hunter
___ solemn *(9)*	m. look for, search
___ hinder *(14)*	n. impede, obstruct, put obstacles in the way
___ urge *(14)*	o. animals that are hunted

Monkey's Argument With Leopard

B. Complete the following sentences with the correct form of the expressions and phrases below. *(Numbers in parenthesis refer to the paragraph number.)*

in search of *(1)*	**take pity (on)** *(9)*
on all fours *(1)*	**give (someone) your word** *(13)*
have nothing to show for it *(2)*	**let go of** *(15)*
in vain *(6)*	**battle of words** *(16)*
so long as *(6)*	**clear one's name** *(23)*
	keep (someone) waiting *(23)*

1. Leopard was a natural hunter. Everyday, he went into the forest *in search of* food, hunting other animals.

2. With nothing to show for all the time he spent waiting to catch an animal, Leopard had waited _____.

3. Predatory animals with four legs, like Leopard, usually adopt a hiding position by crouching down _____ while they wait for an unsuspecting animal to come near enough for them to catch.

4. I'm so mad! I just wasted three hours! I waited on line for concert tickets from 8:00 to 11:00 this morning, and by the time it was my turn, they were all sold out. Three hours on line and I _____!

5. Leopard had always hunted monkeys, so the monkeys believed they were in danger _____ Leopard was alive.

6. Our appointment was for 3:00, but he didn't come until 3:45. He _____ for 45 minutes.

7. A promise is a commitment in words. When you make a promise, you _____.

8. A verbal conflict, such as a debate or an argument, is a kind of _____.

9. Sometimes when people need something from other people, they try to get others to feel sorry for them. They hope the other people will _____ them.

10. His innocence was proven, so now he can _____ and restore his reputation.

11. When we go fishing, we usually _____ all the young fish we catch. We release them back into the water so that they can continue to reproduce.

C. In the story, there are many different verbs for the movement of animals in a specific direction. Each verb has a slightly different meaning depending on how fast or slow and how deliberate (intentional) the movement is. The verbs have been placed on the scale below according to speed and deliberateness.

For the purposes of this exercise, the verbs are in the base form. However, in the story, these verbs are in different forms, except for "wander."

drift	amble	wander	step	rush	race	tear

Slow/not deliberate   *Fast /deliberate*

Finish the sentences below:

1. Leopard went tearing through the forest because _____.

2. Some monkeys were racing each other to _____.

3. The leader stepped boldly to the rim of the well and _____

4. The monkeys all rushed forward when _____.

5. The monkeys drifted away when _____.

6. No game wandered within range while _____.

7. The Tortoise ambled off toward the setting sun after _____.

- *The answers to exercises 3 and 4 are at the back of the book starting on page 70.*

5. Re-telling

Re-write or re-tell the story from Leopard's point of view.

6. Writing and Speaking: Reflecting

A. The Moral of the Story

What is the moral of this story? Is it explicitly stated?
What does the story teach?
Do you believe in what the moral teaches?
What does it mean to "keep your word?"
What do you think should be the consequence if a person doesn't keep their word?
What do you think of Leopard's fate?

B. The Theme of the Story: Values

Would you teach the lesson of this story to your child?
If so, tell or write about how you would teach this lesson to your child.
Would you use different characters?

Tell or write about how you learned the values in this story in your life.

C. The Theme of the Story: Culture

What do you think this story reflects about the culture it comes from?
Tell or write a story from your culture about promises.

D. Related Proverbs

Proverb: *"A promise broken is a friend lost."*
What does it mean? How is it related to the story?
Are there any similar proverbs from your culture?
If so, tell them to your classmates and explain them.

7. Connecting
. . .to another story

Re-read the story called "How Chameleon Became a Teacher."
How would you compare the characters in the two stories?
Which character in that story corresponds to Leopard in this story?
Which one corresponds to Monkey in this one?
Imagine you are Chameleon. What advice would you give the monkeys?
From your direct experience, or from your past observations, tell or write about a
    situation in which you know a promise was broken.

8. Concluding — Symbols and Metaphors

Think back to what you know about Leopards and what you read in the story.
What does the Leopard symbolize in this story?
What does the monkey symbolize?
What does the tortoise symbolize?
Are there any common metaphors for these qualities in your culture?
If so, what are they?

The Gold Ring

Benin

1. Pre-listening

You will hear a story about a powerful king and his youngest son. Before you listen to the story, discuss the answers to these questions:

What does it mean to be humble?
Why is humility such an important quality?
What are some reasons why people give gifts?
How do powerful people maintain their power?
Have you ever lived in a country with a very powerful leader?
Do you believe that young adults should disagree with their parents?
What should a young adult do if they disagree with their parents?

2. Listening

A. **Before** listening to the story, read the following questions.

Did the king think of himself as weak or powerful?
What did the king give to each of his sons?
What did the king make the sons promise to do?
Why was the king angry with his youngest son?
How did the king punish his youngest son?
How did the prince save himself?
What did the king learn?

B. **While** listening to the story listen for the answers to these questions.

After listening, discuss the answers to the above questions.

Finally, listen to the story again.

3. Summarizing

There are some incorrect words and phrases in the paragraph below. Cross them out and write the correct words above them. See the examples in the first sentence.

powerful
Once there was a very ~~modest and humble~~ king. He had seven brilliant sons.

One day, he gave each of them a beautiful gold ring. The ring was a symbol of each

son's loyalty to his brothers. When the king gave the rings to his sons, he said that

anyone who sold the ring would be imprisoned. All the sons praised the king, espe-

cially the youngest son. He said that his father was great, but that the Creator was

the greatest of all. The king was very pleased to hear this, and he decided to honor

his son for saying it. The king planned for the ring to be stolen from the prince, and

then he demanded that the prince find the ring and return it to him in twelve days.

If the prince could not find the ring, he would be sent away from the kingdom

forever. The prince found the ring in a goose that he was going to cook for his din-

ner. When the prince brought the ring to the king, the king realized that he had

been wrong and that he had abused his power.

B. Now read the story and check your corrected summary.

4. Reading: Vocabulary

A. Match the words from the story with their definitions on the right by writing the letter of the definition beside the word. The first word is done as an example. *(Numbers in parenthesis refer to the paragraph number.)*

Word from the story

_e_	magnificent (2)
___	bow (2)
___	executed (2)
___	praised (3)
___	deny (3)
___	humiliated (13)
___	paralyzed (15)
___	gesturing (15)
___	throne (18)

Definition

a. killed; put to death as the penalty for breaking a law

b. dishonored; embarrassed

c. seat where a king or queen sits; power of a king or queen

d. not able to move

e. exceptionally beautiful

f. made very positive comments; complimented

g. not accept; reject; oppose

h. bend forward towards a person to show respect

i. moving the arms and hands to communicate and emphasize speaking

B. Fill in the blank with one of the following words:

unique *(2)*   **ritual** *(6)*   **unpredictable** *(6)*   **shocked** *(6)*   **region** *(19)*   **in vain** *(19)*

1. The king was _____ at his son's behavior.

2. It was necessary to bow at the beginning of the _____.

3. He was so _____. You never knew what he would do.

4. There was only one ring like it; it was _____.

5. Never take the Creator's name _____. It is wrong, and you will pay for it.

6. He ruled over a very large _____.

- *The answers to exercises 3 and 4 are at the back of the book starting on page 71.*

5. Re-telling

Re-tell the story from the prince's point of view.
Re-tell the story from the king's point of view.

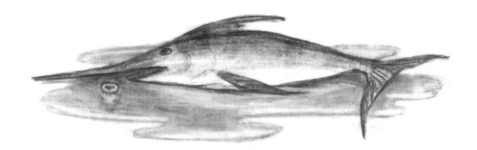

6. Writing and Speaking: Reflecting

A. The Moral of the Story

Which one of the statements below best expresses the moral of this story? Why?

> *Don't put yourself on the level of the Creator.*
> *Too much pride blinds powerful people.*
> *Humility is the key to wisdom.*

What is the lesson of this story? Do you agree with it?

B. The Theme of the Story: Values

What is the theme of the story? Choose the phrase below that you think best expresses the theme of the story, or write the theme in a different phrase.

> *the dangers of excessive pride*
> *the dangers of power without humility*

What are the values represented in the story?
Are these values represented in your culture?

C. **The Theme of the Story: Culture**

What do you think this story reflects about the culture it comes from?
In your culture is humility important?
Are there any stories from your culture about the importance of humility?
Write it or tell it to your classmates.

D. **Related Proverbs**

Proverbs:
> *Power is blind without humility.*
> *Wisdom is the crown of the king; humility is a jewel in the crown.*

What does each proverb mean? How is each one related to the story?
Are there any similar proverbs from your culture?
If so, tell them to your classmates and explain them.

7. Connecting. . . to your own experience

Did you ever receive a very precious gift? Who gave it to you?
Why did that person give it to you? What was the gift?
Why was the gift so precious?
Did you ever give a precious gift? Who did you give it to?
Why did you give it? Why was it precious to you?

. . . to your culture

Describe any special or traditional gifts that men give to women in your culture.
What are the occasions when they give them?
Describe any special or traditional gifts that women give to men in your culture.
What are the occasions when they give them?
Describe any specific or traditional gifts that parents give to children in your culture.
What are the occasions when they give them? What makes them special?

. . . to another story

If you have read the story *"Pearl of Wisdom,"* compare the king in that story with the king in this story. How are they the same? How are they different? How does each one abuse his power? What lesson do they both learn?

Imagine you are the king in *"Pearl of Wisdom"* or *"The Gold Ring."* Write a letter to the king in the other story, advising him not to abuse his power, making reference to the story.

8. Concluding — Symbols and Metaphors

As you answer these questions, think again about why people give gifts.

What does the ring symbolize?
Think again about humility and what it means to be humble.
What does the king symbolize?
Think again about young adults who think independently from their parents.
What does the youngest son symbolize?

54

The Prince and the Orphan

Benin

1. Pre-listening

You will hear a story about a prince and an orphan. An old woman is also one of the characters in the story. Before you listen to the story, discuss the answers to these questions with your classmates.

Does your country have a royal family? Can you think of some countries that do?
Why is the prince important in the royal families of some countries?
Is the naming of children important in your country?
Do you know any orphans? How did they become orphans? Who raised them?
Are stepfamilies very common in your country? How should a family treat a stepchild?
Is there a lot of respect for old people in your country?

2. Listening

A. **Before** listening to the story, read the following questions.

When the prince was born, who knew his name?
How did the king choose a wife for the prince?
Was there a lot of competition to marry the prince?
Who was Hobami? Who did she live with? What kind of life did she have?
How did Hobami's family treat her?
How did they treat the old woman?
What secret did the old woman reveal to Hobami?
What did Hobami do that no one else could do?
What was the result?

B. **While** listening to the story, listen for the answers to these questions.

After listening to the story, discuss the answers to the above questions.

Finally, listen to the story again.

The Prince and the Orphan

3. Summarizing

A. The sentences below form a summary of the story, but they are not in the correct order. Put the sentences in the correct order by writing a number from 3 to 10 on the line next to each sentence. The first two sentences are done for you.

_____ One young lady who wanted to marry him was Hobami, an orphan, with three cruel stepsisters and a cruel stepmother. Her three stepsisters also wanted to marry the prince.

_____ On the day of the contest, the stepsisters were on their way to the palace, when an old woman approached them, asking them for food. They cursed her and continued toward the palace.

_____ So the king decided to have a naming contest at his palace, to give all the eligible young ladies a chance to guess the prince's name.

_1_ A prince was born to a king, but his name was kept a secret.

_____ After Hobami won the contest, her stepfamily was so ashamed of their cruelty to her, that they escaped and became fugitives for the rest of their lives.

_____ To repay Hobami for her kindness, the old lady revealed the secret of the Prince's name.

_____ Hobami arrived at the palace, guessed the Prince's name correctly, won the contest, and married the prince.

_____ Their mother bought them beautiful clothes and jewelry so that they would be attractive to the prince.

_2_ When the prince grew up, his father, the king, declared that the young lady who could guess the prince's name could marry him.

_____ Then Hobami came upon the same old lady and treated her kindly.

B. Now read the story and check your summary.

4. Reading: Vocabulary

A. Match the words from the story with their definitions on the right, by writing the letter of the definition beside the word. *(Numbers in parenthesis refer to the paragraph number.)*

Word from the story	Definition
_____ throughout *(4)*	a. shining brilliantly
_____ orphan *(5)*	b. large crowd of people
_____ starving *(14)*	c. a child without parents
_____ multitude *(26)*	d. great surprise
_____ amazement *(28)*	e. in every part
_____ radiant(ly) *(28)*	g. dying of hunger
_____ conscience(s) *(29)*	h. sense of morality

56

The Prince and the Orphan

B. Fill in the blanks with the words below:

garments   **fugitive**   **chores**   **ashamed**   **implored**   **reveal**
deeds   **obscenities**   **ceaselessly**   **tattered**   **disguise**   **frustrated**

1. The sales clerk saw a man leaving the store with a box, and she mistook the young man for a thief. But when she discovered that the young man had paid for the merchandise, she felt _____.

2. Sometimes celebrities _____ themselves so that people won't recognize them in public.

3. For millions of years, the earth has moved _____ through space, constantly revolving around the sun.

4. He was _____ after many unsuccessful attempts to win the prize.

5. "Please, I beg you, please, please give me some money," _____ the beggar, on his knees.

6. For years they were too poor to buy new clothes, so their clothes were all worn out and _____. They looked more like rags than clothes.

7. Most people only wear their best _____ on special occasions.

8. "The _____" was a movie about a man who was accused of a murder he did not commit. He had to run away from the police constantly until he could prove his innocence.

9. The doctor gave free medical care to the poor and did so many other good _____, that he received a Community Service Award for his generosity.

10. I accidentally hit another car while I was parking yesterday. The other driver jumped out of his car, slammed the door, ran over to me and started yelling _____ at me. I said I was sorry, but he kept yelling.

11. When I was a child, my parents made me do my _____ every day. I had to make my bed, clean my room, feed and walk the dog, set the table for dinner, and wash the dishes after dinner.

12. I can always trust my best friend with the secrets I tell her. I tell them to her because I know that she will never _____ them to anyone.

C. Choose the correct synonym or definition for each word. Before you choose the synonym or definition, look back in the story and read each word in its context. This will help you decide the meaning. *(Numbers in parenthesis refer to the paragraph number.)*

alights *(1)*

> a) shines
> b) comes down
> c) tells about

priceless *(11)*

> a) cheap
> b) worthless
> c) very, very valuable

withered *(14)*

> a) light in color
> b) dry and wrinkled from old age
> c) wide

vanished *(25)*

> a) ran away
> b) spoke
> c) disappeared suddenly

barred *(26)*

> a) obstructed, prevented entrance
> b) undressed
> c) welcomed

- *The answers to exercises 3 and 4 are at the back of the book starting on page 72.*

5. Re-telling

Re-write or re-tell the story from Hobami's perspective.
Re-write or re-tell the story from the old woman's perspective.
Re-write or re-tell the story from the king's perspective.

6. Writing and Speaking: Reflecting

A. **The Moral of the Story**

What is the moral of this story? Is it explicitly stated?
What does the story teach?
Do you believe in what the moral teaches?

B. **The Theme of the Story: Values**

What are the values the story teaches?
Would you teach the values of this story to your child?
If so, tell or write about how you would teach them.
When you were a child, did you learn the values in this story?
If so, who taught them to you?
Tell or write about how you learned the values in this story in your life.

C. **The Theme of the Story: Culture**

What do you think this story reflects about the culture it comes from?
Tell or write a story about kindness from your culture.

D. **Related Proverbs**

Proverb: *"Virtue is its own reward."*

What does it mean? How is it related to the story?
Are there any similar proverbs from your culture?
If so, tell them to your classmates and explain them.

7. Connecting
. . . to your country and culture

Naming:

The prince's name is of central importance to the plot of the story.
What is the importance of naming children in your country?
Who decides names for children in your country?
How many parts are there in a complete name in your language?
What are the parts? What is the correct order of the parts?

Can girls and boys have the same names in your language?
How do you differentiate between boys' and girls' names?

Imagine you are the king in this story. What would you name your son, the prince?
What considerations will/did you make in naming your children?

Do you think children's names should be traditional? religious? common? unique?
Explain the reasons for your answers.

8. Concluding — Symbols and Metaphors

As you answer these questions, think again about kindness.
What does Hobami symbolize in this story?
What do the stepmother and stepsisters symbolize?
What does the old woman symbolize?

Are there any common metaphors for these qualities in your culture?
If so, what are they?

Answer Key

Lesson 1— **How Chameleon Became a Teacher** *page 1*

3. *Summarizing*

Chameleon and Crocodile were good __**friends**__ . They often spent long periods of time __**talking**__ together. So when Crocodile __**invited**__ Chameleon to dinner at his house, Chameleon happily accepted the invitation. But Crocodile was not __**honest**__ with Chameleon. Crocodile told Chameleon to jump into the lake so that he could take Chameleon to his house. But instead, Chameleon __**threw**__ a stick into the lake. Crocodile __**bit**__ the stick, thinking it was Chameleon. When Chameleon saw this, he __**realized**__ how important it was to test Crocodile. This __**taught**__ him a very valuable lesson in life.

4. *Reading: Vocabulary*

A. Matching

__e_ was (very) fond of
__f_ sunbathing
__d_ nodding
__b_ delicacy
__c_ gigantic
__a_ dived

B. Definitions

the effect of something falling in the water	**splash**
shaking with fear	**trembling**
ran away in fear	**fled**
an invited person	**guest**
intelligence, understanding and common sense	**wisdom**

Lesson 2 — *Why Hawk Preys on Chicks* page 5

3. Summarizing

Long ago, all the birds and animals were friends, __except for__ Hawk, who always __preyed on__ small animals and their young ones. Then one day, the animals sent a __message__ to Hawk to tell him not to hunt them anymore. Hawk agreed to stop if the animals could __decide on__ one who Hawk could hunt. None of the animals wanted to __volunteer__ to be Hawk's food, so they decided to have a __meeting__ to discuss what to do. Chicken was the only animal who did not __attend__ the meeting. She had said that she would accept whatever decision the other animals made. So they decided to offer Chicken and her chicks as a __sacrifice__ to Hawk. Hawk accepted the decision, and that is why Hawk preys on chicks.

4. Reading: Vocabulary

A. Use these words to complete the sentences

1. Hawk was the only **exception**.
2. They did not know who to offer as a **sacrifice**.
3. The animals were arriving at the public **arena**.
4. There was much **squabbling** and no agreement.
5. Who should be offered to hawk as a sacrificial **victim**.
6. Shouts of joy and **relief** filled the air.
7. The animals jumped up and down **congratulating** each other.
8. Hawk **promptly** agreed to the decision.

C. Vocabulary for people talking to one another

1. At the beginning of every semester, the President of our college gives a welcoming __speech__ to all the new students. Her __address__ is usually about 20 minutes long.
2. We just had our monthly staff __meeting__, which is always attended by everyone in our department. But next week, we're going to have a special __meeting__ to plan the move to our new office.
3. I really enjoyed Professor Johnson's __lecture__ this morning. Sometimes it's hard to take notes in his classes, but today he was easy to follow, and very interesting.
4. Every spring I attend an annual __conference__ on bilingual education. About 5,000 linguists and educators from all over the world attend.
5. Last night I called an old friend of mine. We had such a nice __conversation__, reminiscing about our high school days.
6. Email is great. People all over the world can have a written __discussion__ about something without being face-to-face. Any number of people can participate.
7. Next spring, I'm going to be a panelist on a __colloquium__ at a conference for English teachers. The subject will be how computers affect language education.

D. "conflict" words

argument	
battle	**war**
debate	**prey on**
fight	**disagreement**

Lesson 3 — *Pearl of Wisdom* <small>page 10</small>

3. Summarizing

  __2__   But one little boy in the kingdom was named Pearl of Wisdom.

  __4__   The king was amazed by his intelligence, so he wanted to know more about him.

  __7__   In turn, the mother of Pearl of Wisdom gave the king an impossible task.

  __1__   Once there was a powerful king who named all the children in his kingdom with ugly, insulting names.

  __3__   He was so intelligent that he won the king's riddle-solving contest.

  __6__   The king decided to punish the mother of Pearl of Wisdom for giving him that name, so he gave her an impossible task.

  __8__   This made the king realize how unfair he had been, and he allowed people to name their own children freely.

  __5__   When he asked his name, and he answered that it was Pearl of Wisdom, the king became very angry because he hadn't named him.

4. Reading: Vocabulary

A. Matching

  __e__ wisest
  __j__ tyrant
  __a__ reign
  __m__ mean
  __h__ pretend
  __k__ exceedingly
  __g__ ignored
  __l__ merciful
  __d__ harvest (v)
  __b__ weeping
  __c__ task
  __i__ clutching
  __f__ seeds

B. Fill in the blanks

You can always count on my brother. When he promises to do something, he always does it. He never __goes back on his word__. He's straightforward with everyone. He never says one thing __behind your back__ and then another thing to your face.

I'm a public defender, a lawyer that represents clients who cannot afford to pay for legal services. I routinely defend people who __break the law__. Recently, I defended a man who had committed a violent crime. I pleaded with the judge not to sentence my client to death. But my pleas were all __in vain__. The judge did not want to __spare his life__. So my client was sentenced to death.

Lesson 4 — **Anancy and the Guinea Bird** *page 14*

3. *Summarizing*

3	He got the idea of asking the Father God to make a new law: whoever does not mind their own business by asking questions will die.
8	He provoked Anancy. Instead of minding his own business, Anancy asked a question about Guinea Bird.
6	He was the only one who had food when everyone else was starving.
1	There was a terrible drought in the land where Anancy lived, so there was no food for anyone.
5	So Anancy got fat by eating them as they died.
2	Anancy had to think of a way to trap some food for himself.
4	Anancy got many animals to ask him questions....
7	Guinea Bird realized that all the animals would die if Anancy continued, so he decided to trap Anancy....
9	As soon as Anancy asked the question, he died....

4. *Reading: Vocabulary*

A. Matching

f	chipping		i	bald
h	grunted		e	majestically
g	fatal		c	ignore
d	trap		b	fade
a	trickery			

B. Fill in the blanks

1. The sudden movement or shaking of the land is an __**earthquake**__.
2. Large areas of trees are burned in a __**forest fire**__.
3. An extremely large wave or series of waves in the ocean is a __**tsunami**__.
4. The violent and fast movement of wind in a circular motion, is a __**tornado**__.
5. When rocks ... fall down the side of a mountain, they produce a __**landslide**__.
6. Violent tropical rain combined with very severe winds ... is a __**hurricane**__.
7. When there is no rain for a long time..., there is a __**drought**__.
8. When the land is covered by too much water. there is a __**flood**__.
9. An explosion inside the earth ... is a __**volcanic eruption**__.
10. When large amounts of ... snow slide down a mountain, they produce an __**avalanche**__.

C. Exterior or skin   Animals

	Exterior or skin	Animals
a.	shell	turtle, lobster, clam
b.	fur	cat, dog, lion, tiger
c.	scales	snake, chameleon
d.	hide	cow, goat
e.	feathers	bird
f.	skin	pig, human

Lesson 5 — **How Goat Moved to the Village** *page 19*

3. *Summarizing*

One day, Goat was baking sweet potatoes, when Hyena __**came along**__ . Goat __**offered**__ Hyena some food but he quickly __**discovered**__ that Hyena wanted to eat him, not the food. Hyena __**feared**__ for his life, so he thought of a strategy to __**buy time**__ so that he could find an escape from Hyena. Goat's strategy was to eat his sweet potatoes slowly. While Hyena was waiting for Goat to finish the sweet potatoes, Lion __**arrived**__ . Lion said he wanted Goat to finish eating so that Hyena could eat Goat and he could eat Hyena. Hyena __**realized**__ he was in terrible danger, so he __**ran away**__ . Lion __**ran after**__ him. Goat saw that this was his chance to __**escape**__ the jungle, so he went to live in the village.

4. *Reading: Vocabulary*

A. Matching

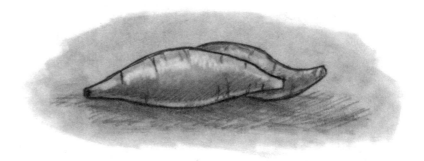

_f_	harvest
_i_	ashes
_e_	bite
_h_	struggling
_a_	clawing
_c_	howled
_d_	chewed
_g_	fierce
_b_	numb

B. Fill in the blanks

1. just in time
2. help yourself
3. itching to
4. all over
5. blood-chilling
6. once and for all

64

Lesson 6 — **The Greedy Father** *page 23*

3. *Summarizing*

3	All the young men of Nadjo's village proposed to Gbessi and offered gifts to Nadjo.
4	Nadjo and Gbessi rejected all the young men.
11	Shocked at her husband's transformation, Gbessi tried to escape from him.
2	He wanted to find a husband for Gbessi because he wanted a high bride-price.
8	Monkey married Gbessi and they went to live on a farm.
12	When she finally got to Nadjo's house, she turned into a monkey as he watched.
1	Nadjo, a poor man, had a beautiful daughter, Gbessi.
7	He convinced Nadjo to let him marry Gbessi.
5	Monkey heard about the beautiful daughter and the greedy father.
10	He suddenly turned himself back into a monkey.
13	This broke her father's heart, and he soon died.
6	Monkey's friends gave him lots of presents and made him very wealthy.
9	But farming was hard work, and Monkey soon got tired of his new life, and missed his life as a monkey.

4. *Reading: Vocabulary*

A. Matching

i	crumbling		h	compound
j	endure		k	grimaced
f	interminable		d	withered
g	realize		b	heartbroken
c	driven		e	insane
a	thickets			

B. Definitions

groom: at a wedding, the man who is getting married

bride: at a wedding, the woman who is getting married

spouse: husband or wife, general word for either gender

wedding: the ceremony that celebrates the first day of a marriage

propose: ask a woman to be your wife, or ask a man to be your husband

bride-price: the amount of money paid to the woman's father by the man who wants to marry the woman

marry: enter into a legal union with a person in order to become his wife or her husband

marriage: a formal relationship with a person, as his wife or her husband

C.   Fill in the blanks

My fiance and I are planning to get married next year. He **proposed** to me last summer and I said "yes" immediately because he is the kind of man I have always wanted to **marry**. He is generous, intelligent, creative, and hardworking. Both of us have large families, with many brothers and sisters, so we're planning a big **wedding** in the garden of my uncle's country estate. Although the minister of our church will perform the wedding, we are planning to write our own vows. We want our **marriage** to be a long and happy one. I'm not planning to dress as a typical **bride**. I'm going to wear a non-traditional wedding gown that I designed. But my fiance wants to be a typical **groom**, so he'll wear a tuxedo. He's more traditional than I am.

D.   Select the correct synonym or definition

1.   **Countless** young men proposed to Gbessi.
     c) Very, very many; too many to count

2.   The young men offered **provisions** to Nadjo as part of the bride-price ...
     b) supplies of food

3.   Gbessi was a very **obedient** daughter.
     a) did exactly what her father wanted her to do

4.   Nadjo was very **greedy**.
     c) never satisfied and always wanted more and more

5.   Monkey brought **gorgeous fabrics** to Nadjo.
     c) very beautiful, b) textiles for making clothes

6.   Monkey brought **priceless** gifts to Gbessi and Nadjo.
     c) extremely expensive and valuable

7.   Monkey said that all the gifts he brought were only a **token** of his love for Gbessi.
     c) a small part of something big

8.   Monkey missed **chattering** with the other monkeys in the jungle.
     a) talking happily and rapidly

9.   Gbessi ran **swiftly** away from Monkey.
     a) very fast

10. In the end, Gbessi realized she had married a **hideous** monkey instead of a handsome prince.
     a) extremely ugly

66

Lesson 7 — **Why Cat and Dog Are Always Fighting** *page 30*

3. *Summarizing*

8	So they decided to consult Monkey.
4	While searching, they suddenly smelled some fresh cheese.
10	Cat and Dog blamed each other for losing the cheese to Monkey, and since then, they have been fighting.
6	Then they stole the cheese from the house.
9	But instead of dividing the cheese equally, monkey ate it all himself.
5	They found the house where the smell was coming from.
1	For many years, Cat and Dog had been best friends.
3	They were hungry and looked for food everywhere.
7	After they got the cheese, they couldn't decide how to divide it.
2	Then one year, there was a terrible famine in their village.

4. *Vocabulary*

A. Matching

j	famine
h	searched
e	aroma
i	sniffed
g	argue
d	ruin
a	scales
c	licked
f	reputation
b	wisdom

Lesson 8 — **A Fisherman and His Dog** *page 35*

3. *Summarizing*

Cross out the incorrect words and replace them with the correct ones.

Don Manolito was an old fisherman who lived in Santo Domingo [**San Juan**] with his donkey [**dog**], Taino.

Don Manolito had many [**no**] close friends, including [**except**] Taino. Taino always followed Don

Manolito everywhere. Nobody [**Everybody**] in the town was accustomed to seeing Don Manolito and

Taino go to the seashore in the morning and return in the evening. One day, a terrible

tsunami [**storm**] occurred while Don Manolito was out at sea. Taino waited on the seashore for

Don Manolito to come back from fishing. But when Don Manolito did not return, Taino

swam out to an island [**a rock**] off the shore to wait for him. Fishermen went out to where Taino

was, but when they arrived, they saw that Taino had been transformed into ice [**stone**].

4. *Vocabulary*

A. Matching

  __d__ hut
  __g__ broken-hearted
  __h__ ashore
  __b__ dawn
  __a__ amazement
  __e__ dismay
  __c__ overwhelmed
  __f__ testimony

B. Matching

disappeared: **vanished**
losing brightness; darker: **dimmer**
being very violent: **raging**
an electrical explosion in the sky: **lightning**
very tall; very high : **towering**
beach; the land next to the sea: **shore**
carried by a powerful force : **swept**

Lesson 9 — *How Yogbo the Glutton Was Tricked* *page 40*

3. *Summarizing*

   10   When Yogbo woke up and took his drum..., the drum sang no more.
   3   She became thirsty and stopped to drink water from a hole in a tree.
   7   In the meantime, Yogbo went from village to village ....
   1   Alougba was a hard-working little girl....
   11   Yogbo realized he had been tricked and escaped from the village.
   4   When her hands got stuck in the hole, Yogbo freed her hands.
   5   But then he put her inside his drum.
   2   One day she got more wood than she could carry.
   8   One day Yogbo went to Alougba's village....
   9   Alougba's parents offered him... an enormous amount, and then he fell asleep.
   6   While Alougba was inside the drum, she sang a song....

4. *Vocabulary*

A. Matching

   i   chore
   e   foolishly
   a   drenched
   b   desperate
   k   plunged
   c   helpless
   h   trap (n)
   l   reached
   j   captive
   d   cunningly
   f   harsh
   g   fled

B. Fill in the blanks

1. **keep up with, left behind**
2. **patch up**
3. **demanded**
4. **common sense**
5. **marvel**
6. **got stuck**
7. **glutton**

Lesson 10 — **Monkey's Argument with Leopard** *page 45*

3. *Summarizing*

__3__ A group of monkeys were playing near the well and heard him calling for help.
__11__ In order to convince Tortoise, Leopard jumped back into the well.
__8__ Monkey was very angry at Leopard for deceiving him.
__1__ One day when Leopard was hunting in the forest, he accidentally fell into a well.
__5__ Leopard promised the monkeys that he would not hunt them anymore.
__10__ They told him their story, but Tortoise did not believe them.
__7__ When Leopard got out of the well, he grabbed Monkey.
__13__ Leopard is still waiting for Monkey to come back and rescue him again.
__2__ Immediately, he started calling for someone to come and rescue him.
__4__ The monkeys came to the well and saw how serious Leopard's situation was.
__6__ Finally, one monkey rescued Leopard because he believed Leopard's word.
__9__ While Monkey and Leopard were arguing, Tortoise came along.
__12__ Monkey and Tortoise left Leopard in the well.

4. *Vocabulary*

A. Matching

__i__ glisten
__o__ game
__h__ flaming
__k__ plunge
__l__ predator
__e__ vanish
__j__ strife
__c__ mercy
__g__ ignore
__d__ faint
__m__ seek
__b__ prey
__a__ solemn
__n__ hinder
__f__ urge

B. Complete the following.

1. in search of
2. in vain
3. on all fours
4. have nothing to show for it
5. so long as
6. kept me waiting
7. give your word
8. battle of words
9. take pity on
10. clear his name
11. let go of

C. Suggested answers. Other answers may also be good.

1. Leopard went tearing through the forest because **he was hungry**.
2. Some monkeys were racing each other to **the top of the tallest trees.**
3. The leader stepped boldly to the rim of he well and **looked in**.
4. The monkeys all rushed forward when **their leader looked in the well**.
5. The monkeys drifted away **when they knew their enemy would die**.
6. No game wandered within range while **Leopard lay in wait**.
7. Tortoise ambled off toward the setting sun after he **waved goodbye to the monkeys**.

Lesson 11 — **The Gold Ring** *page 51*

3. *Summarizing*

                powerful
Once there was a very <u>modest and humble</u> king. He had seven brilliant sons. One day,

he gave each of them a beautiful gold ring. The ring was a symbol of each son's loyalty to

    father   **lost**
his <u>brothers</u>. When the king gave the rings to his sons, he said that anyone who <u>sold</u> the

              executed   **except**
ring would be <u>imprisoned</u>. All the sons praised the king, <u>especially</u> the youngest son. He

said that his father was great, but that the Creator was the greatest of all. The king was

       shocked   **punish**
very <u>pleased</u> to hear this, and he decided to <u>honor</u> his son for saying it. The king planned

for the ring to be stolen from the prince, and then he demanded that the prince find the ring

                       seven
and return it to him in <u>twelve</u> days. If the prince could not find the ring, he would be

      ~~**executed**~~   **fish**
<u>sent away from the kingdom forever.</u> The prince found the ring in a <u>goose</u> that he was

going to cook for his dinner.

4. *Vocabulary*

    A.   Matching

      <u> e </u> magnificent
      <u> h </u> bow
      <u> a </u> executed
      <u> f </u> praised
      <u> g </u> deny
      <u> b </u> humiliated
      <u> d </u> paralyzed
      <u> i </u> gesturing
      <u> c </u> throne

    B. Fill in the blank.

       1. **shocked**   2. **ritual**   3. **unpredictable**   4. **unique**   5. **in vain**   6. **region**

Lesson 12 — **The Prince and the Orphan** *page 55*

3. *Summarizing*

<u>4</u>   One young lady who wanted to marry him was Hobami, an orphan, with three cruel stepsisters and a cruel stepmother.

<u>6</u>   On the day of the contest, the stepsisters were on their way to the palace, when an old woman approached them, asking them for food.

<u>3</u>   So the king decided to have a naming contest at his palace, to give all the eligible young ladies a chance to guess the prince's name.

<u>1</u>   A prince was born to a king, but his name was kept a secret.

<u>10</u> After Hobami won the contest, her step family was so ashamed of their cruelty to her, that they escaped and became fugitives for the rest of their lives.

<u>8</u>   To repay Hobami for her kindness, the old lady revealed the secret of the Prince's name.

<u>9</u>   Hobami arrived at the palace, guessed the Prince's name correctly, won the contest, and married the prince.

<u>5</u>   Their mother bought them beautiful clothes and jewelry so that they would be attractive to the prince.

<u>2</u>   When the prince grew up, his father, the king, declared that the young lady who could guess the prince's name could marry him.

<u>7</u>   Then Hobami came upon the same old lady and treated her kindly.

4. *Vocabulary*

A. Matching

<u>e</u>   throughout
<u>c</u>   orphan
<u>g</u>   starving
<u>b</u>   multitude
<u>d</u>   amazement
<u>a</u>   radiant(ly)
<u>h</u>   conscience(s)

B. Fill in the blanks.

1. ashamed
2. disguise
3. ceaselessly
4. frustrated
5. implored
6. tattered
7. garments
8. Fugitive
9. deeds
10. obscenities
11. chores
12. reveal

C. Synonyms and definitions

Choose the correct synonym or definition for each word.

alights   b) comes down
priceless c) very, very valuable
withered b) dry and wrinkled from old age
vanished c) disappeared suddenly
barred   a) obstructed, prevented entrance